This House That

Also by Peter Grandbois

The Girl on the Swing and At Night in Crumbling Voices

The Glob Who Girdled Granville and The Secret Lives of Actors

Wait Your Turn and The Stability of Large Systems

Domestic Disturbances

Nahoonkara

The Arsenic Lobster: A Hybrid Memoir

The Gravedigger

This House That

Poems

by

Peter Grandbois

BRIGHT
HORSE
BOOKS

For Tanya

Contents

Acknowledgments

After the Pause: "Had I loved better" and "The way a weed endures"

Chautauqua Literary Journal: "Let us also breathe"

Cimarron Review: "In the country of the undone"

Cleaver Magazine: "Unfinished"

Communion: "Everything inside us opens"

The Cortland Review: "As if any of it mattered," "No longer the field," and "The open door"

Diode: "The field in thistle"

DMQ Review: "These days of mismatched socks"

Dunes Review: "And is this mine," "At once the dawn," "[Sometimes I dream us walking]," "Sometimes I think I'll never leave"

Fixional: "Before bodies cool," "Excerpts from the book of rain," and "I often dream of a house"

Fourth River: "No going back" and "What the walls know"

Hotel Amerika: "You are my first darkness"

The Inflectionist Review: "The forest between" and "As if somewhere a fire"

Litbreak: "Killer," "The last death of Captain Nemo," "Nests, secrets, and splintered floors," and "[This isn't the play]"

North American Review: "I'm like a story that someone told"

Nottingham Review: "This small burning"

Popshot: "This world no deeper than the eye"

Random Sample: "There is a prayer that enters every house" and "What waiting has to teach"

Saranac Review: "What silence builds dark" and "The years we lived in solitude" (in slightly different form)

Whiskey Island: "Night Prayer" and "Prayer to keep the door ajar"

Special thanks to the following people for reading parts of this manuscript: David Baker, Mike Croley, Jane Delury, Betsy Johnson Miller, Joshua McKinney, and Margot Singer.

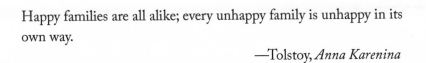

Happy families are all alike; every unhappy family is unhappy in its own way.

—Tolstoy, *Anna Karenina*

I

[I often dream of a house]

I often dream of a house with doors I cannot open
from the inside
A house where I am forced to stare at the barking odor of being alive
A house where I can be in a room inside a room inside a room
because it's safe
A house where I invent things so that nothing real can happen
A house in a field
A house where the thing I love most is not guilt
A house where you are gone and not gone and gone and not
gone
A house where pain does not float like cast off shoes
A house where the sweet past sleeps in jars
A house where neither of us has a speaking part
where we settle for hours without ghosts
where memory folds tight
where our bodies crawl through frayed sky
the two of us holding each other
like walls

Three little pigs redux

You do not build a house with bricks.
Their only job is to show how long
time takes to become visible.

You do not build a house with wood.
Its hour is fixed by the first nail.

You do not build a house with sticks.
They tend to let any animal in whose din
will drown their certainty the world will end.

You build a house with voices
pitched like an angry wind.

And surround that house with fields
of gas-soaked kindling and one long night
that never unwraps itself.

Now close the windows and lock the doors.
You know what's coming.

And is this mine

this fever-tide of summer
with dogs, cats, and children nagging
in and out my front door,

> whole nights spent listening
> to the graveyard-whine of raccoons
> fighting for grease on my backyard grill.

And is this mine, this ceiling
fan that never stops spinning,
churning memories like dust

> until I can almost see the river
> receding from your eyes as your body
> opens to mine.

And what about this dried and broken
leaf I sweep from the floor and out
the door like another's grief,

> as if it could live anywhere else,
> as if it could somehow belong
> to this sun that eats the sky

the silence so violent
it stops mouths from wanting,
knowing things unspoken

> can turn to one more explosion
> in this little book of days we pretend

to read, afraid, as we are, of coming
to the end.

And the things that aren't there,
are they mine, too, like rain
from last night's storm,
like the words we'll never say

        to each other, the things
        we'll never do, the way I wanted
        to hold you as if we could share
        breath with the wind.

I think I know the answer,
sometimes, when I lie across
this deep plain where nothing is,

        except the night in which you
        and I live, except the ache
        in which we both take part,

except the fact that no thing
is ever alone the way
water running over stone

        takes a little bit of stone
        with it, every time.

Night prayer

Come kiss me
           keep safe
my childhood
           unfist the leaves
curled
           in the rented dark
and tickle
           my back
with endless fingers
           so I no longer need
to repeat my name
           until I shut my eyes
finally, please
           close the door
tight
           to keep whole
this broken room
           of stars
and make no sound
           as you tip toe
down the hall
           so I can believe
in the emptiness
           around which
we gather.

Hands

"God enters through the wound."—Carl Jung (1875-1961)

Little holes
We walk through

Out of our bodies
Into ruins of night

Little wounds opening
Wide as morning

Into an asylum
Beyond words

As when your distance
Cuts my hands,

As when your silence
Inches the hammer nearer
To my feet,

As when a woman explodes,
A glass rose,
In the name of God

Here are those hands,
Like little eyes,

Begging for something
To change

Sometimes I think I'll never leave

because snow dusts the driveway without fear of the sun's reprisal

    and I can't solve the window's geometry of rime

because the spider's web beneath the foot of the basement stair keeps
coming back

    and I can't remember where I live

because too many mice have already come to grief in the crawlspace

    and the ends of my shaved beard spill over the edge
    of the sink like blackened footprints

because deep within the furnace looms a yellowed dome of light

    and my hands are too cold to open

because beneath the laundry pile lie wings of silence
reminding us

    of our fall

Before bodies cool

1.

Gravity is the way we fall
together.

2.

The center of mass somewhere
between

3.

Do you know where we're going?
Round and round and round and

4.

My face next to your face next to my face
until

5.

There is no being alone.

6.

Except, we are alone.

7.

Hands with which to touch

matter accreting,

8.

Lips eclipsed.

9.

The sweep of your body across mine pulls my ribs from me

10.

The transit of mine across yours peels skin from bone.

11.

It's difficult   to know
which of us   carries
the greater mass,   which
exudes   the greater
force.

12.

Once, I thought you were the black hole Cygnus X-1,
and I was Sirius.

13.

Now I'm not sure.
Each of us able to swallow

the other.

14.

And we spin, and we spin,
never taking the other in.

15.

This house
that is the axis
of our orbit.
This house
where there is
no room
through which
we can move
together.
This house
in which
we'll never be
apart.
This house
that terrifies.
This house
that deifies
all we have been
to each other.

16.

The beauty of it, our friends say.
The joy of it, our families say.
The radiance of it, our neighbors say.

17.

It's like there's a string
tied to our ankle
the other end to a stick.
This   life.

18.

"What do you want to do?"
"I don't know."
"And you?"

19.

If there is   a darkness,
then something must shine from it.
Is that not so?

20.

If there is   a night,
the sun is a scar in the sky.
Isn't that right?

21.

This slow star weaving,
can't be the journey.

22.

This mathematics
of love is not
the way home.

23.

Whatever   we are looking for
scattered   long ago.
Whatever   we are looking for
never left   this place,

24.

this region that is shaped
like a tear,
a tear
through which
we travel.

25.

And we spin, and we spin,
never taking the other in.

26.

If our stars stood still,
would the house tremble,
the bed shake?

27.

Would our children sing
of stinging silence
flitting from room
to room?

28.

These children like planets

that circle us,
keening through the kitchen,
blasting through the bath.

29.

These children we swallow
in our wild orbit.

30.

Maybe there's no music
but static, the background
radiation of a distant
night

31.

And light sucked from one to the other.
And light ripped from me to you or you to me.
And light. Let's not forget the light.

32.

"Don't hang up on me."
"Don't yell at me."
"Don't tell me what to do."
"Don't patronize me."

33.

There is no room to which we can move,
no place where we can still
this frenzy of moons.

34.

Sooner or later this violence will pull us apart,
this violence that binds us
together.

35.

From a distance, we look like one,

36.

that longed-for distance as tenuous
as dying light.

37.

Made of such dense matter
we have no choice.
The infinite static
sings through blood and bone.

38.

It is better to live like stars
than stone.

Isn't that right?

39.

And we spin, and we spin,
never letting the other in.

Nests, secrets, and splintered floors

I stand at the edge
of this shattered house
grief thickening like
nests of hair, secrets
turning eyes to stone,

and I can't begin to
decipher the strange
writing, the star charts
composed on crumbling
walls and splintered floors.

I don't dare touch
the cracked foundation
with fingers of rain,
not knowing what I'd do
if it washed away.

We have all woken
frightened in the night,
listening to thick
drops of falling bees,
trying hard to blame

the lightning, when if
we'd waited until
morning we'd have seen
the design laid out
before us, the only
primer we need
to begin again.

Let us also breathe

If I have built a web of tongues alone
on this road; if I've reached the fatal point
where I've become a too traveled landscape,
fault lines no longer hidden in my face;
If I am an astronaut un-tethered
from your dream and slipping swiftly out to
distant seas, then we've lost our star-soaked voice.

The silence stinging my mouth was never
the silence suturing yours. Let go the dawn.
Let go the burning face. Let go the hands
bent with what lay unspoken. If you could
know my name, I could see behind the door
in the wave. If you could find your way through
our separate suns, I could find my way home.

No going back

This is the country of unaccustomed
silence. We dare not give it time to take
root. Better to wag about with fevered heads
to wander out of woods begging for food
or redemption under a sunless sky.

It is the country of cast off bodies
that float for years avoiding the touch of
unnamed gods who never cared anyway.
The country of saints with muddled visions
whose child hands have forgotten how to hold.

Perhaps there are two countries, and the line
between them easier to get lost in
than a dream. Little is known of the hard
hours beneath the surface. Less still is known
of the hungry wind above, why it sits

like a cat on a broken fence, waiting.
I once had a dream in which everyone
piled everything we loved into a vast
parking lot then set fire to it and watched
the way it burned beneath a hushed rain.

I wish instead we would've built a field
where sunlight touches every inch of ground.
I don't know why I have this other dream,
or why it's always evening in this country,
only that all things must move to their end.

II

[This isn't the play]

This isn't the play I thought I was in, I say, when I go to bed, again,
without you. It's not the part I was first offered, I tell myself as I lie
awake. The next morning, during yet another round of make-up sex,
I try out my new lines, playing with the rhythm, deepening the tone.
Do you find me more a-ttrac-tive when I e-nun-ci-ate each word? We
smile, knowing how short the scene will be.

    This afternoon, for the first time in a week, I sit down eager to
write. A minute later, both German Shepherds paw at the door. I let
them in and nearly retch with the smell. "Stupid dogs!" I yell, as they
stand there gagging and hacking, frothing at the mouth. "I'm tired
of you!" I shout, as I slam cabinet doors, searching for the elixir that
will rid them of the skunk smell. "I can't do this anymore!" I cry as I
scrub them in the bath, toweling them off with rough hands. They turn
frisky, nosing between my legs, rolling about the floor, barking for me
to join in. How easy it is to play when we don't understand our parts.

Love poem

I could never be more
than these recycled words
written on the parchment
of a floating dream, never
find an end to all that is scarved
in ice beneath a winter moon.

Then you moved through the dark
center of me, and the clouds
couldn't help but shape us
toward rain.

Please tell me it's only the leaves
crying through snow tufted trees,
say it's not you standing in that
frozen field, the wind whipping
the flames in your soot black hair,
and you shouting, always shouting,
at me to ignore the weather.

Winter Elegy

Where is the snow
when I'm feeling this cold,

and where the bitter pull
of silence

Where is the ice
that crusts the road

when I've lost control
of the car

Where is the house
that hides the stars

that hang far
above a dying fire

Where is the bed that held
my sleep

and the dreamed gate and the wings
unfolding my tattered desire

All night I shouted in the field
and where were you

Only when we turn away do things flicker
back

Only when we let go do we remember
the untouched shapes and unheard gasps

of our unuttered lives

Unfinished

If I opened my eyes
from this pretended sleep,
I wouldn't be salting
the driveway before dawn,
though the snow stopped
and the air's no longer freezing.
The trees would speak their silent
part. Swallows would arc
through the brightening sky.
And we would not be as we are.

It's late, and I'm fighting
to stay awake, meaning
all I do is unfinished, meaning
the night is long and dreaming
is as slippery as a fish, meaning
those trees aren't silent at all.
I only need listen
to their deep body ache. Meaning
only in sleep can I hold
my tongue.

What skin remembers

The moment I raised my chest
to your mouth,

a surface filled
with sky.

The night you slept
beside me,

your long limbs a flight
of omens.

The time you said we
must never apologize,

a river of stone
swallowing itself.

The day I lost the map
of us,

secret charts of the world
behind your eyes.

Regret furrows into flesh
revealing what it knows,

what the body refuses
to let go.

This small burning

Except when every word is a betrayal
>Think of the night, how it gathers its children

Except when my grief grows voiceless
>Think of a desert sky so vast it's not really there

Except when I wake and know my dream wrote me
>Think of the sea, how it forgets what it has lost

Except when I see myself in the river's depths
>Think of when the world was rain

Except when I stand before the open gate
>Think of the field with its wild hunger

Except when I come back grown
>Think of my hand on the hollow of your breast

Except when I lie awake guilty that others sleep
>Think of the small burning in this attic room

Except when I tear through this paper house
>Think of how we fall because we can't let go of the wind

Measure

Almonds scattered across an end table.

Snow from a branch as an owl takes off.

The way dawn scribbles out the night.

Juice dripping down the tip of your finger.

No one said there was a limit to all things. How was I to know you would never hold me that way again? So tight I would feel the definition of me.

Every single thing reminds me of the girl you once were. Every thing becomes a word. In a language I no longer understand or speak.

This gate stuck.

This lock jammed.

This book I will never be able to read.

Even if you open it, I have no way to step inside.

Prayer to keep the door ajar

The half-open gate leading through this widowed world

        So if she should grow up

The whisper on the other side of stone, a murmur woven into home

        If she should grow old

The double clutch of wind that pins the dark to the end of this edge-less day

        If she should grow wings that never take hold

The room of trees in which those we clothe are disposable

        So if she should grow tall

The field of mud and dawn curving dead like winter branches

        If she should grow thin

The loose sun on which straw is spun into cold and crumpled clouds

        If she should grow bark instead of skin

And you say this isn't all bad, not bad at all, really. Look, at the stars within

And I say this dark roll of sleep holds nothing but cheap trinkets and baubles that break

And if I wake trembling and alone to find she is not yet grown, let me pray I will say what I mean, pray for empty light in which to see how things start. Not end.

Had I loved better

I used to think the world was inexhaustible, that lovers would always kiss with fingers, that dreams would never be tied into little bundles and packed away in grottos at the end of a long river. I was so sure I wouldn't live at the edge of things, the dust covered and dirty sheeted edge where copper dawns and curling dusks hide the light knifing low across tendons and stillness grows inside us the same way darkness grows outside.

Then I look at you, my son, sprawled upon the bed as if it were another shore, as if it were possible to lie in another dream where hope doesn't scar like an old wound, and I think so what if there's no second world as long as I can keep you free of the serrated light of this one.

I'm like a story that someone told

It's like the desperate whine of wheels stuck in snow, like trying to come up with an ending for the tales I tell my ten-year-old son in bed at night, tales of brigands and pirates, men who are proud of their plunder. No matter what I say, the ending falls short, and he wants another.

So I unravel again, neither of us any closer to listening.

In the country of the undone

This morning my ten-year-old son showed me a drum set he'd made.
     He told me not to count the tape he used to hold things together.
     I told him not to count the days we hear the silence.
     He told me not to count the paper plates he'd cut up.
     I told him not to count the trees growing inside us.
     He told me not to count the beer bottles he'd emptied in the sink.
     I told him not to count the prayer of sunsets.
     He told me not to count the broken pencils on the kitchen table.
     I told him not to count the books whose pages we turn anyway.
     He told me not to count the plastic spoons bent and weeping.
     I told him not to count the leaves buried under snow,
          the many rooms longing builds,
          the life we might have lived under another sky,
          the final depths of blue.
My son told me the name of his band is "The Recyclers."
I told him not to count, ever.

The last death of Captain Nemo

There is a place where my son waits for me. A place where he dreams himself, where shadows are not sewn fast to the hard ground, where he can name each and every demon riding the waves, where he easily steps into

The deep filled with maelstroms and giant squid

where we watched *The Beast from Twenty Thousand Fathoms*, arm in arm on the old orange couch

of Atlantis and Antarctic ice shelves hiding lost

worlds of lizards, snakes, and stinkbugs we hunted until

snow tunnels led us through dusky nights to frozen forts we could defend for days

This is an attempt to sound the midwinter ice, to step from the shore where I'm trapped between one thought and the next. The shore where I cannot drown the incessant coughing of strangers, cannot silence the lover's voice that floats on the other side of hours. The shore where the dead wait to scrape the rime from my eyes, which is why

this is only an attempt.

Killer

I used to have a face but life is brief and I'm starting to lose
now there's only this dripping of words like

     Father
     Husband

at least I know better than to look too closely
last night I caught a glimpse of him
in the mirror

he walks before me now
past the window where I write
dressed all in black
looking back through the pane
at me

his alibi airtight

III

There is a prayer that enters every house

Silence wide as rain
as the wind shuts
our eyes again.

Shadows fall straight
through trees and we

become a world
burning in the dark.

Lifted in the curl
of your finger, I

know only the bloom
of being unhomed,

not this sleep-torn wound
not this night of crows
not this absent moon.

No matter the season

Who stands against me when I pretend
I no longer love you, day after day,
the way a settling house creaks
when no one is listening?

Who keeps watch when I drink whiskey
before bed then turn out the light
and away from you, the way a child
mixes water with dirt until both are lost?

Who speaks of better days when I return
from a long walk and pet the dog
while you wait by the door, the way a creek
murmurs no matter the season?

In what hour will we give account
when each minute pushes us further
from each other?

Only by seeing from afar can we find
ourselves, the way black birds gathering
at dusk tell their story once you walk away.

The years we lived in solitude

How else to explain

    the flash of your face

like breath on the lip of a leaf

    the carnage of dandelion

fluff strewn about the grass

    your hands clothed in morning

mine empty as smoky light

    the story of us held

in a bed of trees we must tend

    storm clouds unfolding

while the streets are still warm

    cobwebs trailing from your fingers

echoes that never end

Everything inside us opens

How else to explain your voice like an ocean inside, desire spilling over a porous shore? Maybe I'm Aeneas playing out the same impossible choice. I sail for Italy not of my own free will. Maybe the night is the silent sea we sail through and dreams the dark circle of birds we become. No beginning and no end. Only tacking across the thin surface of this life until there is nothing left to mourn but stars pressed into the semblance of sky, until we abandon even the most distant figures on the horizon, until the water is enough.

What waiting has to teach

1.

I am for you when night
breathes over the tall grass
where we bathed our pure feet.
I am for you when light
fills our mouths with holy
names we scribbled on tongue-
drenched skin. I am for you
the way a hand can look
like so many fingers
singing the fire's secrets.
I am for you the way
the ocean grows inside
us whenever we lay
down in a field like stars.

2.

"Fuck off!" I shout, throwing my hands in the air as if the bees

could never carry the morning's profusion of lavender through the
open window.

"I don't know why we married," you say. "You were different when we
married."

The ceiling fan churns, understanding the need for dust.

"What about us? The kids?"

The slanted light of morning was never made of silence
but of echoes like a prayer of swallows howling their way home.

"I don't know."

The sun's folded hands open and close, open and close.

"Do you know what it is you want?"

The floorboards creak as I stumble through the half-light on my way
to the bathroom too groggy to pay attention to the wind outside, the
wind inside, the wind moving through me, the wind whispering

"Not this. Not this. Not this."

3.

The way light slows as it enters a body,
knowing we are nothing more than cells
dividing, the way sun strikes a dew-soaked
wheat field, each blade glistening until each
exhausts itself with its own solitude,
or the way a child's hands gather that same
light, as if it knew to shape a window
through which to view the coming dusk that threads
through everything we do, the dusk framing
the door, cutting off the center of all
we knew—*you are not who you are*—and then
the moon, as if anything can be caught
in this deepening dream, as if we could
travel through feathered night and never change.

These days of mismatched socks

Once I was a poem about an overturned sock drawer.
Now it's impossible to separate what's real from what's not.

The morning water encircles me until I'm half buried
in mud. A mountain lake between this world and the next.

The afternoon sun warbles across the sky like a lover
dreaming of slippery things, and I wonder if I am less

empty than the day before, this honeyed song like a sentence
blossoming in my hand until I'm cocooned in echoes

of clouds at night, pulling the thread from my mouth and tying
it to yours, weaving the new moon on a moth's wing between us.

I would choose this world if I could see the difference between
a leaf and a leaf, but how do we move from one life to the next

when neither of us will let go? How nice it would be to stay.
As if we could root in the hornet's wing. As if eyes remained

closed in darkness, as if one hand could sing another's song.

What the walls know

I could be
anything else,
a murmur
beneath cold
sheets, skin stung
with winter's
lie, a story
of a lover
in paint-smeared
clothes.

Yesterday,
I was a house
for rent
crippled from
the sudden
reversal
of us.

Today, I
am a beggar
climbing
your veined road,
though the land
remains level.

Tomorrow,
a mouth shaped
like a long
beak, prodding

and turning
the earth, as if
I can recover
my need
to surface.

[Under every]

Under every deep
a lower deep
opens until
we slip through
fractured sleep
and again
become part
of darkness

Under every sky
a voice rolling
across desert,
bouncing over
rocks, driven
by cruel wind
until mouths fill
with nothing

Under every house
a room of abandoned
stories that sit
like old chairs
losing their stuffing,
waiting for someone
to gather all
that has been lost

How to remain
who we thought we were
when memory's rain erases

each and every track,
washing away the simplest
days when all we wished
for was to be carried
across the water.

This world no deeper than the eye

These old hands like fragile words
break the moment we try to hold
this dream woven from mulberry
smoke and moon-soaked silence.

These tired arms like water
pooling on a rock darken
and dry as soon as we try
to claim the delinquent sun.

We mistake the sighs of trees
for rain, the stirring dust for wind,
as if falling leaves could stop
the horizon's stagger.

You tell me this music can hold,
but I say we have forgotten
the song, or at least the words
we used to drum up memory

that feathery sky that flies
somewhere between the clock's tick
and the ear behind your eye
looking for some place to be found.

The way a weed endures

If nothing of the past remains
except what we remember, then

why this shame that never stops
filling holes

why this bearded man walking about
the house asking his own name

why these leaf-brindled rivers
clogged with yesterday's pain

why can't I find a sharp enough
blade with which to write

each and every note of blame
we owe to ourselves

why does it take so long to become
human, the way a weed endures

the rain. So long? No. Not near
enough. Not nearly long enough.

The forest between

being and not is
night flies from my head
and I'm left trying
of your hand in mine
me while I slept or
what trees say and
not enough to stroll
or across a grave
not nearly enough
over a white field
from a mountain top
of this book and those
what we see outside
see inside settles
perfect shroud if you
if you could only
within that forest
offer you leaves
would point to the wet
smile then fade like rain

slipping the same way
the moment I wake
to recall the feel
as you sat beside
thought I did between
what they fail to say it's
straight through a spare dream
with an empty hand
to scatter flowers
or to collect clouds
between the pages
of the next between
ourselves and what we
a fog that forms the
could only lie down
sift through wet grass deep
where if I could I would
and if you could you
curls in your hair and

How we might touch

When the wind that began our days whips its way
toward an impotent tongue

    and the imagined smoke that hides our names
    rises to moan

When the air laden with lies grows thick enough
to carry

    and the corners of the field are found floating
    on frigid waves

When we are left with too few strings to lead
us from our martyred song

    and mouths too small to bleed

Then we shall know our distance, how it will stretch
only so far before the stars

    in their perfection are forced to intervene
    and lay down along the horizon,

until what lies between us goes unseen.

As if any of it mattered

Move the way a spider moves, tiptoeing across the bathroom floor, without the need to get anywhere.

Weep with the silent swell of stone.

Feel the way smoke rises in gray radiance. The way lush thunder rolls past the storm-soaked earth.

Speak the way wind threads through a crow-laden field. The way the paper-white bark of the birch peels like breath.

Watch the milky night of winter from a backward facing seat.

Learn to balance shadows, like memories, on your finger.

Imagine a world where we can invite the other in.

Believe there is no end to that world.

No anchor mooring us to this one.

IV

No longer the field

but the cave where you and I gather, the cave that is my eye, the eye
that dares not look into the corners of things, corners that haunt the
gaps within our lives, that fall upon us like the dead, and the stairs that
lead us there, unseen stairs running through layers of drunken light,
through gardens of briars and brambles. Sometimes I imagine us play-
ing there, or praying. It's the best I can do. And some things must be
done, even with the danger of getting lost, again. Besides, maybe that
prayer will sound like whale-spout, and maybe that spout will carry us
not to another field but to an ocean where we never need blur beneath
the raking light of our desire.

He remembers undressing her

We saw it coming
The swarm of stars
Cooling inside us

Moon pale as a hand
Over the darkened water
Of our blood

And yet we did nothing
But welcome memory—
That stammering sea

That only opens
With ghost words—
And listen

To our growing old,
A covenant of bones
And breath we keep
With ourselves

As if somewhere a fire

Winter sneaks in while I sleep.

The chainsaw whines through wood
as if it knows the trick of suffering.

Deep in the dream,
I bundle myself in layer upon layer,

as if I can carry you with me.

Nearer the surface,
the murmuring of bees
my desire,

like broken sky
over the softening snow,

like every thing, we pray.

I am a sleepwalker, slipping
through your house.

I turn the corner and
there you are,

as if somewhere a fire.

You are my first darkness

Let us start with the fact
that our days have detached as if
the sun had forgotten its dreams.
Let us end with the act
where the trees are redeemed.
as if all things still had a voice.
Let's talk of a river where
choice rests behind each rock,
as if cold might still the blood.
Let's count each ruddy spark
that rises and churns like prayer,
as if we could see through night's
bankrupt air, not where we are
but where we wanted to be.

Excerpts from the book of rain

The dogs have stopped barking

Throats thick with dust and pain

And every drop of every storm that has ever been
lives on my tongue, asking why

I saw you once and nearly drowned

The rain gathers us in its arms and carries us bound
to the sea

Because words float away we should let the sea speak first

Look at the thirst of my hand

See my hand open and close

How it knocks on the door, as if sorrows,
like crows, could scatter at the hint of a storm.

The open door

If there is a dream where all of our hands
are birds and all the light that falls from us
pools into magnesium fields through which
we fly, let us break for uncharted lands.

If there is a place where the smoke of rain
rises from stone steps and the spider sits
watching the trees sing of their emptiness,
let me not slip and fall, grasping your name.

If there is a time where the autumn wind
rises and falls like breath under the sound-
less moon, let me pray for a small, feathered
anchor to hold me to your painted skin.

If there is a blue where the broken sun
burns through leaves smaller than hands unfolding
to take us from the calling water, let
me open to the gift of your ocean.

If we have arrived on this ancient road
like a mountain loon returning in spring,
let us rid ourselves of crippled grammar
so that we may walk with a lighter load.

If there is a door small enough to fit
in a finch's eye and wide enough to
hold a newborn star, let us wait for it.
We've nothing but time, and our love, to lose.

At once the dawn

All my life, I have tried
to find my language
in the dank earth,

to follow the seasons
in their infinite
capacity for pain,

to see you through a
window instead of
hands shut like doors.

Once, I'd like to open
to the chance voice of the
cricket in the dark, listen

to the lowest thing, to trust
that the thunder inside is
no battle but a blooming.

[Sometimes I dream us walking]

I know a place in the forest
where owls' eyes listen to rain,

and sometimes I dream us walking
there, but moss is shallow and

branches so fierce in their need
they forget—nothing that leaves

stays found. So let me be the first
to step into this distant wood

and speak: Here is my body.
Here is the rain.

What silence builds dark

Anything can be made
of a house

ground down to gravel

rusty nails hammered to stars
studding the sky

a shard of tile the grief-
stricken moon

carpet tacked overhead
the cold night

the ghost of bricks
from once solid walls
mortared into trees.

Don't wait for your window
to come.

The field in thistle

Both thorns and thistles it shall grow for you; and you will eat the plants of the field.

—Genesis 3:18

There's no sign of the path through the field
The path to the window
The window with darkness waiting behind
The darkness that listens to the sleeper
The sleeper with fish in his blood
The blood that knows the answer to the riddle
The riddle that opens the fevered hand
The hand that is about to strike

Thistle's down and thistle's thorn,
we wake slowly but are quickly worn

There's no mote in the wind to follow
The wind split in half by a blade of grass
The grass that sews shut the mouth
The mouth filled with names like flies
The flies birthed from silence
The silence that scrapes the night
The night that balances on bitter nettle's bloom
The bloom that stings no matter the season

Thistle's down and thistle's thorn,
we die slowly but are quickly born

What is it we give to each other?
What is it we fail to heed?

Where are the walls? The windows?
Where are the ceilings and floors?
Why do we need?
Why does the wasp nest beneath the eve
        continue to grow?
How do we come in from the cold?
How do we forgive ourselves
        without growing old?

Thistle's down and thistle's thorn,
we love quickly but are slowly torn

There's no way to name this desire
The desire of dead sparrows beneath the pane
The pane on which broken branches cry
The branches bare except for thorns
The thorns that prick until we feel the loss
The loss that weaves a prison from the thistles
The prison that opens to a field
The field that promised to lead us home

About the Author

Peter Grandbois is the author of seven previous books including, most recently, *The Girl on the Swing* (Wordcraft of Oregon 2015). His poems, stories, and essays have previously appeared in such journals as *The Kenyon Review, The Gettysburg Review, Boulevard, Prairie Schooner, The Denver Quarterly, New Orleans Review, Zone 3*, and *DIAGRAM*, among many others, and have been shortlisted for both Best American Essays and the Pushcart Prize. His plays have been performed in St. Louis, Columbus, Los Angeles, and New York. He is senior editor at *Boulevard* magazine and teaches at Denison University in Ohio.

CPSIA information can be obtained
at www.ICGtesting.com
Printed in the USA
LVHW090553250122
709218LV00008B/650

9 781944 467050